SOULFUL

DAILY REMINDERS TO UPLIFT
& NOURISH THE SOUL

JOY BRISBANE

© Copyright 2025 Joy Brisbane

Published in the United States by Hill of Content Publishing

Published in the United Kingdom by Hill of Content Publishing

Published in Australia by Hill of Content Publishing

Published in India by Hill of Content Publishing

Distributed by Etoile International Group. Hong Kong.

hillofcontentpublishing.com

PO Box 24 East Melbourne 8002 Victoria Australia

All rights reserved. No part of this publication may be reproduced, stored in a retrieval system or transmitted in any form by any means without the prior permission of the copyright owner. Enquiries should be made to the publisher. Every effort has been made to ensure that this book is free from error or omissions. However, the Publisher, the Author, the Editor or their respective employees or agents, shall not accept responsibility for injury, loss or damage occasioned to any person acting or refraining from action as a result of material in this book whether or not such injury, loss or damage is in any way due to any negligent act or omission, breach of duty or default on the part of the Publisher, the Author, the Editor, or their respective employees or agents. The Author, the Publisher, the Editor and their respective employees or agents do not accept any responsibility for the actions of any person - actions which are related in any way to information contained in this book.

National Library of Australia Cataloguing-in-Publication data:

Brisbane, Joy,
Illumination

Includes index: ISBN: 978-1-7637882-1-3

DEDICATION

To my children

Tania Brown and Robert Bell

Through you I have seen the beauty of contrast
For you my love never wavers
Because of you I have grown

I have been blessed

FOREWORD

Simply listening to the news or glancing at each day's headlines feels like the world is spinning out of control. It can leave anyone feeling disillusioned, fearful, lost and exhausted. There is no doubt that we are all being faced with what feels like endless uncertainty that extends from the local to the global and can dampen the spirit as we struggle to live with purpose, love and belief.

While we all face our personal challenges, it is clear that we need daily reminders to uplift and inspire us to keep us walking towards the light; to live with more love and less hate; and to embrace less fear and more belief.

Soulful speaks directly to the heart and the soul, taking us on an inner journey to uplift the mind, the heart and spirit.

This book serves as a powerful reminder that if we want to live fully, we need to tend to the matters of the heart and the soul as we continue on the daily journey of living our best lives.

Gregory Landsman

*Ecstasy is not of the heart
But of the soul*

Joy Brisbane

AUTHOR'S NOTE

The intent I held in my heart as I set about creating this book, was to bring a message to ponder upon.

When we stand in the truth of our soul, our divine spirit, we stand in the light of divine grace and love - both from within us and from the beautiful ones in spirit who walk beside us - those magical beings of light. From within that place of our divinity, our sacred soul space, we are capable of creating whatever journey in life we desire.

May you enjoy your journey and relish in the experiences of your soul.

Blessings... Joy Brisbane

SOULFUL

LISTEN TO THE INNER VOICE

OF YOUR DIVINE SOUL

FOR IT HAS GREAT WISDOM

No path

Leads to nowhere

All paths

Have a purpose

LIGHT

Where there is

Light

Darkness

Cannot exist

The drumbeat – the heartbeat
All are one, all are one
A pulse out – a pulse in
Ancient as earth
Older than fire
Thrumming with water
Carried by air
Season on season
My heart's drum – your heart's drum
Heart and soul – body and mind
Cosmos and me – planets and suns
All are one - all are one
The drumbeat – the heartbeat
All are one – all are one

DECISIONS

Ultimately we
And only we
Are responsible
For the decisions we make
And their outcomes

Journey
Beyond the safety
Of your comfort zone
And discover the essence
Of whom you truly are

SOULFUL SEEKING

All that you seek is not around you

It is within you

Remember who you are
Know you not that trust is the key
To creating all that you long to be
You have the power; you are the way

WITHIN OUR SOUL

When we concentrate on our physical welfare and survival and place our greater importance on material wealth and success then we take ourselves away from our true essence

We are denying the greatness within our soul

Peace and harmony

In the world

Begin with

Peace and harmony

Within self

LIGHT AND LOVE

Ecstasy is not of the heart
But of the soul
It is that moment
Of absolute emptiness
Where there is no thought or feeling
And the space opens to be filled
With the pure energy of profound joy
Of total connection to spirit
Then you understand
This is who you are
This light, this love
This complete and fabulous you

The greatest treasure
We have
Is the beauty
Within our soul

ONLY YOU

You and only you
Are the greatest creator of your life
You are unlimited potential
Begging and craving to be discovered

We all have

A giant within us

That is powerful

And eternal

SELF LOVE

To love self
Means accepting self
For whom we are
In this precious moment of time
To accept self
Means loving self
For whom we are
In this precious moment of time

True and lasting power
Comes from
Wisdom
Compassion
Understanding
And Love

PEACE AND PASSION

Peace and passion
Are a powerful team
With peace
Comes detachment from need
When need is absent
Passion is intensified
True expression of passion
Is in the giving not the wanting

What flows out from you
Comes back to you – every time
Put out anger
Anger you will receive
Put out love
Love you will receive

SELF WORTH

Work towards releasing all negative thoughts and feelings toward self and others - they open up a space to be filled with self-worth, forgiveness of self and others, higher levels of integrity, honesty, and love

Be the beautiful soul you are
It is enough

ENLIGHTENMENT

The choice is always ours —
To knock on the door to enlightenment
Or keep it firmly closed

We are the great creators of our own lives

*Within the physical world we create what we
believe we are worth
and we have the potential to bring into our lives
abundance in all its forms*

*Within our mental and emotional lives
we have the power to heal
and to recreate ourselves*

*Within our spiritual soul-selves we already have
the greatness waiting for us to discover our true
essence - our divinity*

LOVE

*One becomes truly wealthy
When we open our hearts
Not only to the receiving of love
But also to the giving of love*

*The little boy picked me
a bunch of flowers; mostly weeds.
With the blooms came a gentle kiss.
'These are for you.
The blue ones are like the sky,
and the yellow are sunshine.
The white ones are the clouds.
There are no grey flowers
so I can only pick you happiness.'
His little eyes sparkled.
I hugged him and closely whispered,
'I love you too'.*

TRUE EQUALITY

*True equality comes when those
who know they are great
can begin to see
accept and nurture
the greatness in others
by willingly sharing
what they have discovered
within themselves*

*Honour your physical body for it is the vehicle in
which your soul can be present in this world*

*Love who you are
all of you
for there is no other like you
No other who can think and feel as you do
Whatever negative thoughts
you have about yourself
become the alchemist
and change the negative
into the positive*

*Create what is right for you not
what others may wish for you
Become the master of your life*

LISTEN WITHIN

Take time out to be with I, me, and myself
To listen to the inner voice of
your divine soul
For it has great wisdom

When you stand in truth
when you see what is right for you
when you let go of expectations
from and toward others
and when you begin
to live your life from within you
from your source of light and love
rather than seeking the approval
of the outer world
then you begin to
taste the deliciousness
that comes with freedom
the richness of being
true to your soul

LISTEN TO YOUR HEART

Listen to the voice of your heart
— your feelings
The mind and its thoughts
can bring you into confusion
but your feelings never lie

*Give up trying to live up to the
expectations others' have of you*

Live to your expectations of Self

YOUR PRECIOUS JOURNEY

Stop being a slave in pleasing others at the expense of denying your own precious journey

Only respect for each other, acceptance of our uniqueness and individuality, acknowledging the right of each person to be who they came here to be, and tapping into the source of light and love that lies within our gorgeous souls – only that can bring an end to the destructive journey of the ego

SELF VALUE

It is a beautiful thing to be present for others and to do things for them that bring them pleasure and joy

But when you do it to gain their admiration and favour then you become imprisoned by the need to be accepted and noticed

Miracles don't happen from the head space

Only through the connection to the heart and soul can we manifest miracles

Open the door and welcome home your true Self your own divinity

DIVINE SELF

*When we choose to get to know
our deeper divine self
we begin to find the light of love*

*Discover what is your truth in your
spiritual journey
Always there will be those who want you
to walk their path
Often they believe it is the only path
There is never only one path to the top
of the same mountain
Walk the path that is right for you
There is no right or wrong
There are only differences*

THE POWER OF LOVE

*Love is a far greater power than that
of retaliation and resentment
Within us all is the greatest of powers
– the power of divine love and creation*

We are both light and dark
Without the darkness
Which is our teacher and challenger
We would not fully appreciate
The divine light within us

HEAVEN WITHIN

We find heaven within when we become connected

to the special and unique energy of our divine soul

We are the ones that create the
Burden in our minds and hearts
We are the ones that block our
Way forward through fear
It is us who become stubborn
Trying to do everything
From the energy of thought
Rather than allowing things
To unfold naturally and quietly

REVERENCE

*Sometimes what we know to be true is a
precious gift to be held in reverence
and not shared with others*

*Sometimes life deals out tough experiences
closing doors to what has been
and opening new doors to what can be
so we may grow and expand
into our soul's energy of greatness*

VOICE OF THE SOUL

The soul has its own voice

if we care to listen

*We always have a choice to
walk in darkness or
to seek out the light*

Always

BELIEVE IN YOUR DREAM

Hold on to your dreams
What you believe you create
It may take fifty years of patience
But eventually
– if you truly believe in your dream
It will be realised

Not all shoes fit the same feet

Walk the road that is best for you

TRUST IN THE SOUL

Imagine what it would be like

if you could fully trust

in the power of your divine spirit

You are great beyond your imagination

Tough situations often open doors for

new explorations of the self

AWAKEN TO A TRUTH

The word enlightenment means...
To enlighten
To bring light onto a subject
To allow one to see clearly
To awaken to a truth

*You may feel trapped within the physical world
but no one can take your thoughts
and feelings from you*

*Use them to prepare for a future
you cannot yet see*

PRECIOUS

*Hold close to you that which is precious
and don't always expect others to
understand or agree with you*

There are many mysteries for you to uncover
Trust in your intelligence and remain adaptable
Be flexible and trust in your instincts
As you move forward in preparation
For your new future

LETTING GO

When we let go of old patterns
That stop us from moving forward
We open the door to rebirth
And the magic of new creation

When opportunity knocks

Open the door

You never know

What awaits on the other side

INEXPLICABLE

There are some things in life that can be explained

and there are certain things that can't

*Creating a fulfilling life can be hard work
but when we learn to trust our guides
and trust our own intuition
following what we know to be true for self
then will we discover
the magic of co-creation*

THE BEST TEACHER

In all forms of work the best teacher is experience

*Experience not only teaches us about our role in
service to others through our work
it can also bring us into a deeper understanding
of self and the gifts we bring to others*

*No person nor anything from our outer
world can fulfil us
Fulfilment comes from an inner journey with self
When we learn to love self
When we truly know we are enough
Then we find fulfilment from within*

HONOUR YOUR TRUTH

Honor your truth and live it
Never compromise who you are
To keep others happy

Make time to meditate

Through meditation we can find an inner well of

deep stillness and peace that can nourish our soul

and deepen our connection with our true selves

DIVINE ESSENCE

It is often difficult to look at our own soul
And come into acceptance that
Within all of us
Exists the essence of the divine

A smile and a soft word of caring or praise

can break down barriers very quickly

MASTER OF MY SOUL

One day...

I will become the master my soul longs to be

Exploring the vastness of a cosmos

Whose grandeur is beyond

My wildest imagination

I am human

I am spirit

I am all - and I am nothing

I am that I am

YOUR GIFTS

Never compromise your gifts

To be loved or to fit in

*Transitions and transformations
can be painful experiences
We don't always see the lessons and the blessings
that come with such necessary states
for us to grow beyond who we are*

*Nonetheless they can be invitations
to stretch ourselves out of our comfort zones
so we may discover more of who we truly are*

RESILIENCE

*You are more resilient
than you know
or can imagine*

*There is nothing to compare with actual life
experience when it comes to saying to someone
— I understand*

*Those two words take on a different energy
a greater depth of integrity when the person
speaking to them has had a similar experience*

RISE AGAIN

*Once you hit rock bottom
there are only two ways to go –
leave the planet or begin to rise up again*

*Enlightenment is not a one-off experience
It is an ongoing awakening
With our connection to our
Soul-self and the realm of spirit*

OUR SHADOW SIDES

Facing our shadow sides opens us up
To the delicious light within our souls

*As I travelled into many cultures
one thing became clear to me
people are just people*

We all hurt, cry, laugh, rejoice, and
search for our true identity

*At our deepest core
we are all one of the same*

INNER WEALTH

There is no material substitute
for the discovery of one's inner wealth
the journey of the soul
toward sublime happiness

*All souls ultimately lead back to the same hub
the same point in time and space*

*They all lead back to source
back to Great Spirit and
the unity of oneness*

QUIETUDE

Take time out for quietude

and to look inwards

We are pure energy and have the potential to explore the universe in all its greatness and incomprehensible glory

DEEP WITHIN

*Go deep within
And find the stabilising force
That resides inside all of us*

*Clairaudience is French for clear hearing
Claircognizance is French for clear knowing and
understanding
Clairsentient is French for clear feeling
Clairvoyance is French for clear seeing*

CONSEQUENCES

Positive actions create positive results
Negative actions create negative results
All actions have consequences

Embrace the innocent child within you
And step into the greatness
Of the energy within your soul

BE STILL

Be more

be still and

find that deep peace

that simply IS

*When the mind rules our lives
and the ego dominates
we become separated from the beauty
energy and voice of our soul*

PEACE AND REST

We find peace and rest in our heart and soul when we let go of the negative aspects of our journey with our Human Self and we no longer need to feel bigger and better than others

The power of ego says – look at me
I am great and you are less than me
The power of our divinity says nothing
– it simply IS

WHEN WE ARE READY

As much as we may want to 'save'
the whole world and enlighten people
we will only touch those
who are ready to be touched

Growth of any kind cannot be forced

It is not for us to try and push someone towards our beliefs

It is our place to gently guide them into a deeper awareness of their own truth

ROSES OR DAISIES

*In our garden of life some
prefer roses to daisies*

*There is no right or wrong
to another's journey in life
there are only choices*

Our outer world reflects our inner world
Our inner world reflects our outer world
As within so without
As without so within

SELF FORGIVENESS

*It all begins with self-forgiveness
and deep honesty*

*Self-judgement and recrimination
only serve to push us into depression
anxiety and feelings of worthlessness*

*Nothing beautiful or nourishing can
grow in such poisoned soil*

Our souls incarnate
Over and over again
In order to grow and
Expand into their greatness

A DEEPER JOURNEY

Where the ego and its need for power resides
There you will find people lost
To their deeper journey with the soul

When we deny our inner journey
Our growth and healing
Our awakening to our true Self
No amount of money and material possession
Can make us happy

YOUR SOUL SELF

*Remember it is not you
the human Self
that is doing the work
but your soul-self
the divine aspect of you*

You won't know the joy of unconditional love, and the beauty of living in a state of peace and happiness unless you let go of all the adult ego-driven qualities that bring about anger, hatred, discontent, greed, lack of worthiness, and mistrust in self and the world

LIVING WITH JOY

Live for the sheer joy of living without
thinking how you can become better
greater or more important
than someone else

Live in simplicity
Be playful and creative
Continue to explore your world
and your place within it

*When we strive to be the ego-driven being who
needs to compete against others and become 'great'
in worldly terms
we open the pandoras box of tension,
disappointments, discontent, jealousy,
and resentment
We walk away from the peace and radiance of our
true Self – our divinity – our heaven*

SEEDS OF POSSIBILITY

Our souls were created in purity

and greatness

We all carry the seeds of possibility

of greatness within us

The need to be right brings only

judgement, criticism, hate and anger

HUMANITY

Without the service to humanity

our greatness is lost

*The heart and its feelings are
also the voice of the soul*

GIVE THANKS

It is time to give thanks
For the job our body does
To respect it
And to move away
From being discontent
With our physicality
To loving and honouring our body
The temple of our soul

*When we become aware of the peace
stillness and loving power
of our divine spirit within
and draw from that well
we will go on to live a
happy and contented life*

EMBRACE WHO YOU ARE

Begin to truly live and not just exist

To just exist is to die to Self

To live is to embrace all of who you truly are

*It is time to open ourselves up to the wonder and
power of our inner giant – our soul*

SOULFUL

We are all here, every single individual across this
planet, to learn one simple lesson - how to live a
joyful and free life from within us
To discover that the source of lasting happiness can
never be found in the outer world
and to embrace our power as a unique
loving and compassionate soul

That is the truth that sets us free

ALSO BY JOY BRISBANE

A CONTEMPORARY INTERPRETATION OF SCRIPTURE

EXCERPT FROM BOOK 1. CREATING HEAVEN ON EARTH

Are you seeking healing for grief, for a heart that hurts, and a mind in turmoil? So often we wander through life, struggling to keep going, hungering for answers, when help is all around us... both in spirit and in our human world.

I am not religious. I have no affiliations with any religion. I am deeply spiritual.

I have always struggled with the concept of there being a single entity called God. How can there be such a being who controls all of the universes, the cosmos? For me, the power such a being would hold would be beyond belief or faith. Science is now proving there is more than one universe, and it will take a very long time for them to investigate our own before they even begin on the others. The extent of the cosmos is beyond our ability to comprehend. How can one being have control over the entire cosmos?

However, I do believe in a collective force of many thousands of beings of a highly evolved nature. This realm I call Great Spirit. And I believe we are all a minute part of that magical and magnificent spirit, for it not only exists outside of us, but such energy is contained within our soul-self. That is the best way I can describe something to which none of us truly have the answers. And my assessment comes from working with these realms for almost sixty years, and the study of highly educated and evolved souls, who themselves have written on this subject for centuries.

I am a psychic medium. I embrace the wisdom of all the great masters who have walked this planet and I am privileged to be able to connect with some of these wise beings in spirit.

To me, a master is a highly evolved soul who has earned the right to be called a master and is not gender specific. There have been many such masters going back from modern times to the ancient ones. Each era brings with it such people who are relevant to that time in history; who are teachers and leaders, healers, and philosophers; people who renew ancient wisdom and make it accessible to the seeker adding, as they go, their own particular understanding of such wisdom.

One of these powerful beings made it clear to me that the time has come for me to bring a different point of view to ancient writings based on his life. Known to Christians as Jesus – he is known to me as Yeshua.

My religious background is that of Christianity. My dad was a lay preacher in the Uniting Church, Australia. As a young person I diligently followed where my dad led me. But as adulthood grew within me, so did the ability to think beyond the confines of religious beliefs and restrictions.

I never was one to be told what I should or should not believe. I have always held strongly to my right to understand what is true and real for me, and to allow all people to embrace the belief that they love. I never could understand why people killed for the sake of religion. And I could never accept that Christianity was the only doorway to heaven, or that any of the religions held the secret to ongoing spiritual existence beyond our human self.

I began to explore many beliefs, finally coming to understand that a walk with spirit was an inner journey that needed no adherence to any organised form, or doctrine, of religion. I remember well the day it dawned on me that religion and spirituality were two different things. They can, and often do go together, as my beautiful mother showed me. When I realised I did not need to be religious to be deeply spiritual – that was the day I was set free to follow my own path, allowing it to unfold before me as I walked with spirit.

Back in 2006, after my husband had died, I was sitting quietly alone in my newly built home contemplating my future, when out of the ether came a booming voice that deeply frightened me. This big masculine voice said, "The time is not now!" It was in answer to a question I had been contemplating about stepping into a new way forward. I am someone who has been used to living with esoteric experiences since I was seven years of age but even for me, that voice left me shaken. To this day I can still 'hear' it and get shivers when I think about it.

Years later when Yeshua came through to me in meditation and asked me to return to the Bible and bring to the people a different understanding of what has been written, of what he said, I momentarily froze. And then I cried. I cried tears of pain for a youth that had been filled with fear and judgements, a youth based on rights and wrongs around a man called Jesus, around the idea of hell's fire and damnation, and the belief that the only way to enter the "kingdom of heaven" was through the doctrine of the church.

Images within the memories of my childhood arose from the dark passages of my subconscious mind. A belt being pulled from my dad's trousers as he prepared to discipline me in the ways of righteousness. Long and cold hours spent sitting on uncomfortable seats as some man droned on about the need to repent of my awful sins. Conversations about the heathen religions that created fear in my heart. The flood gates of childhood memories had been opened. I yelled at him, "You have got to be kidding me! No way. No way will I go back to that time!" And then I heard in the Master's strong, commanding, yet tender voice, "Not only will you bring a different way of thinking about the texts within that book, but it will help you to heal that part of your youth. I will be working with you."

Yeshua is unlimited in all that he does. He never was a Christian. Christianity arrived after his death. He was born into a Jewish family. At age twelve he went through the ritual of gaining his bar mitzvah as Jewish boys still do. The Christ energy is not limited to Christians; it belongs to all people. It is an energy – not a person. It is the energy of love and enlightenment. Yeshua embodied the Christ energy as have thousands before him and since his life. He was no ordinary man, but a highly evolved soul, a master, and a prophet who is just as relevant today as he was two thousand years ago.

I have worked with the writings of the four apostles – Matthew, Mark, Luke, and John – in the King James version of the Bible's New Testament.

May the insights I have gained, by revisiting these texts with a different mindset, help you to come into a deeper understanding of self, of the realm of spirit, and to walk the path that is right for you. No glove ever fits all hands. Follow your own heart, your own truth. There is no right or wrong – there is only enlightenment and love.

There have been moments throughout my life where I have experienced such bliss. When it happens, when I feel the extreme love and support that comes from those in spirit toward me, there is nothing more profoundly magical and beautiful. I - am – in - heaven!

EXCERPT FROM BOOK 2.
ILLUMINATION

We all must find the shoes that fit our feet as we walk our path of spiritual enlightenment.

When I heard my dad say, from the pulpit of the church in which he was preaching, "Today our reading comes from the book of Revelation," I knew we were in for a sermon based on awful visions and the need for redemption of my wicked ways. I would inwardly sigh and prepare myself for fearful thoughts.

To the Christian world, the man who gave the visions to his disciple and brother, John in the last book of the Bible, The Revelation, he is known as Jesus. To me he is known as Yeshua. Why? Because Yeshua was Jewish. Jesus was never a Christian. He was born into a Jewish family by Mary. Christianity did not begin until years after his death.

I adhere to no religion, but I am deeply spiritual. When I was twenty-seven years of age, I walked away from my background of Christianity and the dogma and judgements that went with it. Twenty years prior, I had seen a vision in my bedroom of a beautiful spirit woman. Thus began a life-long journey with psychic ability that led to a place of working as a medium. I am also trained in nursing and Lifeline counselling. The more I have seen and worked with the realm of spirit, the more I have understood that religion is a very different thing to spirituality. They can, and often do, go hand in hand. My beautiful mother showed me that such can be the case. But the man-made rules and regulations that religions adopt, and the fear religions use to keep control of the minds and emotions of the people, were never for me.

If, like me, you have found the last book of the Bible somewhat confusing, and rather terrifying in a haunting kind of way, then hopefully what I uncover will allow you to gain a different perspective on what is going on in the pages of this book, written almost two thousand years ago by Yeshua's disciple and brother, John.

As with my previous book, *Creating Heaven on Earth*, [giving a different voice to the sayings of Jesus], I am writing about The Revelation after an encounter with Yeshua. He requested of me to go back, firstly to the gospels, and then to the last book of the Bible, The Revelation, to give a different perspective to what he had said and what he saw.

I began this adventure from a place of apprehension. My young adult revulsion of this book, created through the teachings of my dad and ministers of churches, still held its power over me. This is not a book I would ever have considered writing, but that compelling and strong soul called Yeshua had other ideas. It was probably because of that actual revulsion, and the intrigue I held as to why anyone would want to read it and believe the preachings that came from it, that brought Yeshua to me with the request, "I want you to write a book based on the last book of the Bible; the book of The Revelation." He knew the rebel inside of me would see it through different eyes.

My husband, who was sitting up in bed beside me at the time Yeshua spoke to me, was shocked when I yelled out to Yeshua, "You want me to do what? No way! I can't. I can't go back into that." Poor Allan had no idea who I was talking to, or what it was about. When I told him, I burst into tears, let go, and quietly said, "Your will be done!"

As I began to read each chapter, trying to make sense of it all, I would quietly say, "I have no idea what I am going to write Yeshua. What on earth is this chapter about? Over to you my friend." And to my astonishment I would begin to see through the old-style language to the pictures, the visions Yeshua was presenting to John. The more I moved into the book, the more I began to see, and it was very different to the frightening and controlling messages of the religious leaders in my youth.

I came to realize, the majority of the prophecies Yeshua passed on to John through the visions, were not so much about our personal journey with spirit.

They were a forecast on the development of the young Christian faith and its churches; the abuse its followers would have to endure; followed by the fall of the Roman Empire; and finally the raising up of the new Jerusalem within the realm of heaven.

However, I also found many gems of self-realization and illumination of my own inner journey. I found a deeper and more personal relationship with the Master. My in-depth study of a book, that once haunted me with its darkness, has helped me to heal a time of confusion and disenchantment with my very religious father and his perception of what the book of The Revelation meant for him.

Beyond the sometimes dark and mysterious visions that Yeshua apparently imparted to John, hidden in these pages will be some amazing and beautiful moments of awakening to a different and profound voice. A voice which, in the past, was often deliberately portrayed by Christian leaders to be a fearful one - to hold us in a place of obedience and contrition. A controlling power wielded to keep us in servitude and ignorance.

I now enjoy being in my latter seventies, and I have become a little wiser than to simply accept what others wish me to believe. The numbers are falling away from the churches, and it is time for them to ask the question – why? Perhaps it is because these books, written two thousand years ago, appear to bear little relevance to our more advanced technological society. A society that can't even understand some of the stories, and doesn't want to be burdened with ancient teachings that seem to be filled with fear. I ask the question, who reads the Bible now except for devoted Christians? And when was the last time such devout Christians studied the book, The Revelation?

Throughout my life, independence and strength have helped me to maneuver my way through difficult times. I value my independence as others would value gold. Independence and the right to be me, to have my own truth and voice, has helped me to walk a path often strewn with obstacles that threatened to bring me down. Those rough times helped me to find my own deep inner power, a power that can only come from my soul and my desire to remain true to who I am.

Through my journey with the Master and John, I have discovered a truth very different to the one my dad embraced. You may agree with my dad, and find my discoveries foreign, and that is perfectly okay. I am neither interested in agreement nor disagreement, only to give you, the reader, an opportunity to think for yourself and embrace what is right for you. Each of us brings to this world our unique perspectives, a thread in the overall tapestry. We all must find the shoes that fit our feet as we walk our path of spiritual enlightenment.

Remember, as we open the verses of this often-strange book of The Revelation, it was written two thousand years ago and has been interpreted into different languages since that time. A lot can get lost from language to language, and we are relying on the perspective of the translator. I am no expert, and this is not another translation. What I aim to achieve in the writings of this book is to extract the gems as I see them and shift the fear from these rather daunting stories.

I would like to demonstrate how translation through languages can change wording and therefore, our vision of the truth. Let us take the Lord's Prayer as an example. The common use of the Lord's Prayer, translated from Aramaic to Greek to Latin to English reads:

Our Father who art in heaven,
Hallowed be thy name.
Thy kingdom come.
Thy will be done on earth as it is in heaven.
Give us this day our daily bread, and forgive us our trespasses,
As we forgive those who trespass against us,
And lead us not into temptation, but deliver us from evil.
For thine is the kingdom and the power, and the glory, forever and ever.
Amen.

Now let's see what the version looks like, translated back in 2015 from Aramaic directly into English:

Abwûn
Oh Thou, from whom the breath of life comes,

d'bwaschmâja
Who fills all realms of sound, light, and vibration.

Nethkâdasch schmach
May Your light be experienced in my utmost holiest.

Têtê malkuthach:
Your Heavenly Domain approaches.

Nehwê tzevjânach aikâna d'bwaschmâja af b'arha:
Let Your will come true – in the universe just as on earth.

Hawvlân lachma d'sûnkanân jaomâna:
Give us wisdom for our daily need.

Waschboklân chaubên wachtahên aikâna daf chnân schwoken l'chaijabên:
Detach the fetters of faults that bind us (karma) like we let go the guilt of others.

Wela tachlân l'nesjuna:
Let us not be lost in superficial things,

Ela patzân min bischa:
But let us be freed from that what keeps us off from our true purpose.

Metol dilachie malkutha wahaila wateschbuchta l'ahlâm almîn.
From You comes the all-working will, the lively strength to act, the song that beautifies all and renews itself from age to age.

Amên
Sealed in trust, faith, and truth. And so it is.

Wow, what a difference. This reminds me of the Chinese whispers we used to play as children. You take ten people and the person at the beginning of the line whispers a message to the one next to them, and so on down the line. By the time the tenth person has received the message it has completely changed. The Bible has been translated several times through different languages. How much have the visions given to John by Yeshua in The Revelation changed through translation? And have they been deliberately changed through the ages to fit with the Christian churches' control over people, using such visions to place the people into a state of fear and obedience?

There is a wonderful saying by philosopher and psychologist Herbert Spencer (1820-1903] that states:

> *There is a principle*
> *Which is a bar against all information*
> *Which is proof against all arguments*
> *And which cannot fail to keep a man*
> *In everlasting ignorance,*
> *That principle is*
> *Contempt prior to investigation.*

As we delve into the hidden secrets in this last book of the Bible, let it be one of revelation and illumination, as we let go of contempt, and open our hearts and minds to a different investigation into the visions given to us by Yeshua.

ABOUT JOY BRISBANE

Joy Brisbane is an author, counsellor and psychic medium. For over four decades she has supported people to experience healing and live their best lives.

To connect with Joy Brisbane go to

joybrisbane.com

www.ingramcontent.com/pod-product-compliance
Lightning Source LLC
Chambersburg PA
CBHW061729070526
44583CB00024B/3065